the SMURFS™

WHO ARE THE SMURFS?

Popcorn ELT Readers

New Words

berry

This is a **berry**.

There are a lot of **berries**.

fly

They can **fly**.

fantastic

This is **fantastic**!

go on holiday

They are **going on holiday**.

2

leader

She's the **leader**!

swim

She is **swimming**.

make magic

She is **making magic**.

wizard

He is a **wizard**.

Where's the popcorn?
Look in your book.
Can you find it?

the SMURFS™

WHO ARE THE SMURFS?

Who are the Smurfs?

The Smurfs are very small. They are blue.

The Smurfs have white **hats**.

hat

finger

They have four **fingers**.

Where do they live?

The Smurfs live in Smurf Village.

There are a lot of Smurfs!

They live in small houses. The houses are **mushrooms**.

mushroom

Who is the leader?

Papa Smurf is the **leader**. The Smurfs listen to him.

Papa Smurf is very old. He can **make magic**.

What do they eat?

The Smurfs eat **berries** – Smurfberries!
They are red.

They eat **nuts** too.

nuts

What do the Smurfs like to do?

It is hot! The Smurfs like to **swim**.

Brrr! It is cold! They like to **ice skate**.

ice skate

Where do the Smurfs go on holiday?

The Smurfs like to **go on holiday**!
They go to the sea.

They **fly** to the **mountains** too!

mountains

Who is Gargamel?

Gargamel is a **wizard**. He does not like the Smurfs.

His cat wants to eat the Smurfs!

Why do we love the Smurfs?
They are funny! They speak Smurf!

And they are ~~fantastic~~ Smurf!

THE END

After you read

1 Match the sentences with the pictures.

a) There are a lot of Smurfs.

b) The Smurfs listen to Papa.

c) The Smurfs like to fly.

d) The Smurfs like to ice skate.

e) They eat nuts.

2 Write the words.

berries   blue   fingers   hats   ~~small~~

a) The Smurfs are s m a l l .

b) The Smurfs have white _ _ _ _ .

c) The Smurfs have four _ _ _ _ _ _ _ .

d) The Smurfs eat _ _ _ _ _ _ _ .

e) The Smurfs are _ _ _ _ .

3 Circle the words to complete the story. Then draw and label the picture.

1 Gargamel / ~~The Smurfs~~ are going on holiday!

2 They are *happy / sad.*

3 They go to the *mountains / sea.*

4 It is *cold / hot.*

5 They like to *fly / swim.*

Then they go home to

S _ _ _ _   V _ _ _ _ _ _ !

Quiz time!

Read the sentences. Answer Yes or No.

		Yes	No
1)	The Smurfs have black hats.	☐	☐
2)	Papa Smurf is old.	☐	☐
3)	Smurfberries are green.	☐	☐
4)	Gargamel likes the Smurfs.	☐	☐
5)	His cat wants to eat the Smurfs.	☐	☐

SCORES

How many of your answers are correct?

0-2: Read the book again! Can you answer the questions now?

3-4: Good work! The Smurfs like you!

5: Wow! Are you a Smurf?!

23

1 Listen and read.

The Smurfs

The Smurfs, the Smurfs!

They're small and blue.

The Smurfs, the Smurfs!

They're your friends too!

2 Say the chant.